CAN YOU HEAR ME NOW?

All The Things They Ignored

List of Letters (table of contents)

' My Intro to Love'

The concept of love to me is no stranger.

But In my mind the word means danger.

Forced to put up walls and shut people out .

Only because past trauma is in my head floating about .

Scared of love and living in fear.

Scared I'll never know the feeling because it's too dark in here .

In my mind, that is.

Where the concept of life itself is only a fizz.

There is no manual on this sort of thing.

I used to think I'd find love with a summer fling.

How could someone with such a big heart be scared of love to her core?

That's because she never experienced true love before.

Not from the one she wanted most anyways.

As long her boys were good love wasn't a thing she'd say.

But I can't blame my mother for her brokenness.

I love her to death none the less.

On this journey, I've realized that love is all around.

In some cases, pushing me until I fall to the ground.

In other cases, lifting me high into the clouds.

My stomach with the flutter flies and my heart beating loud.

So this is love ? All of these mixed emotions?

Does anyone have a bowl for me to hold them in?

My intro to love wasn't swift but rigid.

Looking for it in people I knew couldn't give it .

Why are we all hurt inside ? Maybe this is what love does.

The concept lost in translation because of us?

Hurting one another and calling it the four letter word.

Blaming others for everything that ever occurred .

Can you meet love more than once?

Maybe she's mature now , and not such a dunce.

A class clown, a silly joke ?

No, real love is hope.

Or at least that's what I believe…

Who to thank for introducing love to me ?

My mother? Her "love" was too harsh.

My father? His "love" was too far.

How about my siblings? Their "love" was confusing.

What about drugs? My love for them somewhat inducing.

So who can I say introduced me to love ?

I guess we'll have to ask the mourning doves .

' Frequency '

Lately I feel like I'm vibrating at a different frequency .
Around others I feel out of place quite frequently.
When the pitch gets louder , it does reach a different wavelength.
My metamorphosis is mental.
My inner thoughts are what I give into.
I feel like I'm changing.I'm not always present .
Certain people simply put here for lessons.
What could I learn from them?
How to lower my frequency, down to a hymn?
I've realized my mind has no equals .
It has built walls very few can get through.
And when they do , they are praised.
It's almost like I've longed to be saved .
Lately I have been operating at a different frequency.
Like the Devine himself is trying to speak with me .
Telling me to let go of my pain so I can live peacefully.
Maybe the cords of my heart are finally healing.
After all I'm doing better with talking about my feelings .
Loving myself again so I can love another .
However parts of me still want for my mother .
My vibration's frequency has elevated.
Past traumas are slowly becoming out dated .
As I open myself so I can flourish,
Bits of love and light start to flow back in.
My third eye has began to show me who's real.
The envy is now hard for them to conceal .
They're only here to absorb my energy.
To make me think I'm crazy. My mind the enemy.
But as I again become one with my self,
I realize other frequencies can be harmful to my health.

' Reflection '

Turning on the light, I'm faced with terror.
A distorted face , giving the death glare.
A hole where her heart is supposed to be.
Her blacked out eyes starring back at me.
She must be hurting and in so much pain.
She's cursing and lashing out with so much vein.
She's bleeding from her arms. They're cuts she's made.
There was a heart beat but it's slowly starting to fade.
"Who are you ? What's wrong ,are you okay?"
" I used to look just like you before today."
Her response gave me chills and I reached to touch her.
I'm stopped by a shivering cry for her mother.
"What happened to you ? Who did this?"
"Oh my love. Ignorance is bliss."
I want to help her but she won't let me in.
More cuts on her legs start to pry open.
"Help!" I scream.
"What a wonderful dream."
Why doesn't she care that she's bleeding?!
I stopped for a minute to think.
Who is this girl I'm looking at.
I looked around her. We had the same surrounding.
She smiled as I realize I was staring at me.
A hollowed out shell,
That's been put through hell.
This must be the reflection.
The part of me I'm neglecting.
The room becomes dark and she starts to fade away.
"I used to look just like you before today."
And with that she was gone,
Leaving me on my own.
To weep and cry, wanting to die!
What spell has she cast?!
To where I can see my issues through the mirror glass?!
That was not myself ! How could it be ?!
Yesterday I smiled so beautifully.
I looked at my hands and seen the bones.
How could she leave me here on my own?
They walls began to melt along with my heart!
How did I get in side this place? It is so dark!
I try to scream for help but my voice is caught.
The mirror shatters.
The poor girls blood is splattered.
I lay in the floor wishing she knew how much she mattered.

' A Higher High '

My highs aren't so regular anymore.
They are so intense and leave my brain sore.
Pineal gland open and sensitive.
The vibes are wild and some trips are dangerous.
Looking too deep can bring pain with this.
Be careful what your third eye decides to peep into .
You see things you didn't know were within you.

' Silenced '

Broken. Selfish & alone.
Confused. Scared and not wanting to go home.
But I have no choice and this shit is hurting.
Trust for you is gone and this family thing ain't working.
Replaying the incident which has taken over my heart and mind.
Wondering if I can ever trust you or even forgive you overtime.
That night felt as if it would never end.
Now I have to smile and be happy or at least pretend.
Now the door's locked in hopes it never happens again.
Partaking in drugs and alcohol is how I figured I should cope.
Covering pain with more pain, does it work? Nope.
Surprised I haven't slit my wrists or tied any rope.
Instead I'll cry, sit back , and smoke my dope.
Listening to sad songs of lost love and hope.
Tell me Nigga! How the fuck should in cope?
Forced to keep it a secret and not talk about it.
Brush it under the rug, no matter how I feel about it.
Planning my escape from this dreadful place.
I can't even stand to see your face.
I don't want to be around you or even answer your calls and text.
Figuring if i can keep my distance i can control what happens next.
Maybe I'm remembering it wrong. Maybe it was a dream. Maybe it didn't
happen.
Nah,Fuck that! 'Cause my thoughts are overlapping.
You don't want it out afraid they will question your character.
Begging us to stay to keep your family together.
Fuck this family, and fuck you too!
Not just for that but for everything you put us through.
The reason's gone. But now I'm traumatized.
Now you disgust me and I refuse to look in your eyes.
I was supposed to trust you, what the fuck? you were supposed to
 protect me .
Now I'm holding this grudge in hopes you neglect me.
I'm not sad anymore, I'm just angry.
How could you do this? Control your fucking drinking.
The purest heart has now been torn in two.
Broken, fucked up, and silenced by you.
Fuck you and fuck this silence.
If this gets out it'll end in violence.
Fuck you! This family, your drinking, this marriage.
And fuck this stupid ass silence!!

'Deafening Silence'

Over time I've learned to tune the world out when I wish to be left alone.

Now I'm starting to hate the feeling of being lonely, by myself and on my own.

The silence around me now deafening.

My thoughts are louder and more threatening.

There's always so much going on so I wish for silence.

But I consequently start to overthink when it gets too quiet.

A slave to my mental, but there's no master of my heart.

I feel as if I can only express my pain and passion through works of art.

When I am silent, there is something wrong with me.

I'm most likely thinking, or trying to figure out how to breathe.

Wanting to be free from the chains of mental illness.

I know the hardest stage of healing is going to be forgiveness.

I'll suffer in silence, I have no right to be a victim.

When there are people around me wanting to carry my burden with them.

Am I supposed to find love? Should I look through hues?

Am I supposed to keep going after I've lost my muse?

Losing all will to live and keep fighting these battles.

Becoming one with the darkness, where my mind travels.

I no longer seek validation from those I'm surrounded by.

I just ask for a moment of silence for me, a ribbon in the sky.

If I ever choose to wave the white flag in surrenderance

Let my departure, be a lesson, not a hindrance.

The silence around me now deafening.

My urge to stop fighting is a bit more threatening.

'To My Sister'

A wound healing with angel dust.

A blessing in disguise

And any worthy man's prize.

You are a sight to behold.

A gift wrapped in gold.

A scratch on the surface

Does not make you imperfect.

There are times we go through things

Situations we think would break our wings.

But yours are indestructible,

Making your presence, oh so lovable.

A cure to a cold heart.

You are god's perfect art.

A priceless masterpiece,

Your mind I wish to be at peace.

Diamonds are made from pressure and coal,

So what harm could be done to your soul?

If they cannot see it then they are blind,

You are the sweetest one of your kind.

Don't let them bring you down, Yasmine

For you are so valuable to the team.

Don't worry, all these can be fixed if we believe,

Even your wounded angel wings.

'Session 1'

Feelings of grave euphoria start to take over my body,
As this boy that ain't mine pushes deeper inside me.
I feel like I'm Using sex to cope with stress and anxiety.
Not even taking into account the demons he could be hiding.
No soul ties.No feelings.
Just using him for sexual healing.
This can't be very helpful to my mental.
Cause now I'm always looking for something to get into
Grievances in the back seat that leave my body sore.
I know it's wrong but I can't help to want more.
Asking myself, "Why? Baby, what is it?
Cause you think he's broken and you can fix it.
What about you? Who the hell's gonna fix that?
You can't even stand in the mirror and love what you look at?
No boy can make you feel whole inside.
Because no boy can be a man and swallow his pride.
No, instead he'll tell you to lay back and he'll push your panties to the side.
Not fixing you but fucking you.
Bringing you a smile
That will only last a little while.
When are you going to let yourself heal?!
These feelings you think you have are not real!
Don't you understand you are in pain?
Don't you understand you're a pawn in this fucked up game?!
Society has molded you to have a cold heart.
Now you can only express you're feelings through art.
So tell me kid what the fuck makes you so angry?
Why the fuck do you envision people hanging?!"
Shh! Give me a minute, let me think!
It doesn't help when you yell at me.
I don't think I'm broken. I think I'm reserved.
"Then why the fuck do you keep putting everybody else first?!"
Would you quiet down it's already loud in here.
"Maybe because we're tired of seeing your fucking tears."
Okay, I get it! Would you just calm down?
"You won't be happy until your heart bleeds in the ground.
Stop putting yourself in situations to get hurt.
Cause ain't nobody but I went pick that heart up out the dirt.
Make wiser decisions Trinitee'! You got to think smarter.
Because if it's on God's will you'll one day have a daughter.
Thank you I think that's enough for today.
I think your friend is here for a while I hope she enjoys her stay.

'Empty'

My heart aches from crying
Tears run down my face
While innocent black people are dying.
My heart feels empty and the world feels sad
How come we can't come together for good on my or bad?
Time and time again, one of our own is killed.
And whatever state police department substantially thrilled
Our hearts are now empty
And we have no remorse
As likely the end of the world should run its course
History repeats as we have grown so wary.
Ridding our eyes of tear gas with a product of dairy.
The only crime we've committed is being black.
Naturally, there is a huge target on our back.
Fathers,uncles , brothers, and cousins
Dropping like flies and being killed by the dozens.
I feel only emptiness when they say to make america great.
The color of my skin is an innocent weapon, involuntary fate.

'One of Those Days'

I guess today is going to be yet another day
Where everything including myself feels out of place
I want to cry and hide my face.
Another sleepless night
Not a pain pill in sight
Tossing and turning as if sleep and I were in a fight
Clueless as to what was done
To make me feel so out of the norm
I don't think I serve a purpose in any of your lives
So I'll just sit back and swallow my pride
Sometimes I like being by myself
It just doesn't help my mental health
Anxiety consumes my body
In case you're wondering why I'm acting oddly.
Today I'll overthink every detail.
Wondering if it's lies to me you tell.
Today I won't talk as much
I'll be rather quiet
And if you don't understand why, you might despise it
Today I'll push you away when it comes to interacting
I'll make the silence awkward and long-lasting
It's better if you leave me alone today
I don't want to hurt you
I'm not too sure what I'll say
On these days, I'm a bit sad and kind of angry
I might do things to make you hate me
I'll look out the window
Letting my head fill with sorrow
As time starts to pass
I'll lose focus on the current task
I'm sorry if this made you feel bad in any way
I just wanted to warn you of how I'd act these days

' I want to be healed '

This time around has to be different.
I said I wanted to heal and I meant it.
Even if it takes me every day I'll try to smile.
It might not be so genuine for a long while.
As time continues to go on, I'll finally feel healed.
As the days go by my smile will be the real deal.
I'll find the purpose and time to let this go.
Roll up the memories, exhale them in the smoke.
I know this isn't good but it's helping me cope.
Numbing me to the pain, The pieces that broke.
I don't want to be alone but I don't want to be around anybody.
It sounds weird but it's comforting, oddly.
People take the good in me and leave me defenseless.
So for now I'll hold it back, it's already proven to be too intense.
I'll give this love to myself. And alone I'll heal this broken soul.
Putting myself back together, making me whole.
This time around the walls are built with Titanium.
It'll take a while to get through or even to break them
But at least my heart is protected.
My energy can only be projected.
Not stolen or manipulated.
As time goes on, the love that I give could never be outdated.
I want to be healed. And yes, I do mean fully.
I don't want to be triggered every time I think of things that fooled me.
Protecting myself at all costs.
Accepting all things that I felt I lost.
I know that healing takes time
And now the only heart I have to heal is mine.

' Hiding pain '

How come I feel homeless inside this home?
How come I am surrounded and still feel alone?
I walk into the house every day wishing I was gone.
Nobody wants to hear your feelings
They only care about their own.
So bottle them up and pray life goes on.
So many emotions bounce around and off the walls of my head.
Lately, I've been crying at night wishing I was dead.
The violation cut me so deeply,
It takes hours or maybe days before I eat or fall asleep
Sleeping with the door locked so no one else can come in
Tight feeling in my chest. The emptiness. There's so much pain.
I do my best day in and day out to try and at least stay sane
But the sad world around me seems to have other plans
I want to die!
My head and chest hurt and I can't shake this painful feeling inside
Everybody says they're there, but you're too far to reach
Nobody would notice if I was dead in my room rotting for weeks.

' Trip '

Looking into my own eyes it's evident how tired
my mind and soul have become.
Dreadfully falling from a high, back into reality,
as I fall asleep my trip is done.
Over eight hours, the ticket was just ten dollars.
The next day the rest of the euphoria seeps out
of the pores of my collar.
The rocket's ride was ever so smooth.
Accompanied symphonies bring my mind to
soothe.
Now that I'm sober, the trip is over.
Those same tired eyes face indecent exposure.

' From Your Friend '

What if I told you someone would listen?
That they'd understand what a lot of others didn't.
Someone you could be yourself around.
Someone who'd uplift you instead of bringing you down.
Sometimes we all need a shoulder.
To cry on, as the seasons get colder.
Amid all your troubles, know that you aren't alone.
Know that you have an escape when things aren't great at home.
A safe place to confess
Whatever you need to get off your chest.
A person who will be there whenever you need.
You could talk to me for hours about anything until you felt your mind was freed.
Capitalizing on your pain
Brings me no gain.
I can only imagine what you're going through
With everything that's brought to you.
Know that I'm the person you can talk to.
Whenever things are dark and grey or blue.
I know what it feels like to be trapped inside your mental.
Wanting to let it out but I have no one to vent to.
I know the life you live you're told to be strong.
But how can you hide your pain with so much going on?
You keep intoxicated to ease your frustration.
I know that your opening up comes with great hesitation.
What if I told you I'm in no place to pass any judgment?
Because you were right, sometimes I do cry until my heart's content.
Sometimes we all need to let it out.
It may not change the situation but it could release some doubt.
I can see in your eyes you feel like you have to hold it in.
But now you don't have to. You can talk to me, your friend.

' To My Brother '

We are so much alike with only a few differences.
We aren't slow to anger and we don't care to listen.
 Sometimes we just so happen to overflow from all the anger left within.
However, we've never turned our back on each other.
You are my twin flame, my protector, my brother.
Going through certain things at certain ages,
Has taken our minds on a roller coaster of places.
Shaping us to only show emotion with our faces.
All the times we have laughed and cried
We've even apologized, putting pride aside.
I do believe I'd be lost without you.
I would be hurt and nothing else would seem true.
I appreciate you to wit's end.
There have been times when you were my only friend.
When I feel like sometimes I've lost my birthright.
You'd helped me gain peace of mind even if only for a night.
I am also very proud to be your little sister.
I wanted to be like you. A young gangster.
Thank you for all of the advice and a listening ear.
I knew I wouldn't stay in trouble for long, with you near.
Each day our bond grows.
The new coming in and pushing out the old.
Painting our picture together, the new colors are bold.
It's amazing what pain can do to us.
How close we are now even though we used to fight and cuss.
I just wanted to tell you, that whenever you are down you can always come to me.
After everything we've shared you know, I'll be listening.
I love you to the moon and beyond.
And I do believe she is the one for you.
Maybe because she and I are rather fond

' The Only One '

I'm sorry it took me so long to accept or what you might say realize.

You're the only one I connect to when I'm high.

High on love, high on drugs, high on you, or high on the lows of pain.

You're the only one I'm with and I feel sane.

I read these words to you with love and little hesitation.

With my heart I want you to be the destination.

You're the only one that loves every flaw of mine.

You should know I'm here no matter the time.

You're the only one I think about.

I wish I was in your mind, day in and day out

I vent to you about my psyche journeys.

And you continue to try and learn me

The only one I want to cry to.

The only one it hurts me to lie to.

You are the only bright light in the darkest corners of my mind.

I hope in me it's love, peace, and joy you find.

I want to be the only one for you as you are for me

'S E X'

Building bonds through sexual relations.
When you're inside me you take me through fazes.
Sex is my new release.
Depression is just as deep.
Only you make me feel better.
As I grip onto you, my insides wetter.
Adjusting to your size
As I release my demise.
This drug has become my new high.
My eyes roll back as I grip you.
With you close to my ear singing your blues.
In these moments I'm yours and you are mine.
Even if it's just a short time.
Passionately kissing both sets of my lips.
Going harder and faster as you grip my hips.
Telling me not to run and to take it.
Your body's the blunt I love to hit.
My mind drifts into euphoria, it lands in a different dimension.

' I feel fat '

I cried when I looked in the mirror today.
How could anyone love me if I look this way?
I feel fat and unpretty.
No one should have anything to do with me.
My sides are too wide. My hips go in too far.
My back has rolls and my butt isn't up to par.
I feel fat. My boobs hang too low.
I tighten my bra so no one will know.
I wonder what they think of me during sex.
"She should probably stop eating, she's a fat mess. "
I wish my waist was slimmer. My chest 2 cups smaller.
I wish I could vividly see the bones on either side of my collar.
I wish my butt was rounder and sat up higher.
I wish my hips spread a little wider.
I wish my arms weren't so flabby.
How could people possibly look at me?
I think other women are so beautiful.
Then I look at myself and say what a fool.
Do you think guys are attracted to you?
I look in the mirror and I HATE what I see.
How could someone possibly love me?
I cried today because I feel fat.
I feel unpretty. Why isn't anything changing that?
My insecurities make me believe his love isn't real.
Maybe I just have wounds that need to be healed.
But HOW could he love me and I look like this?!
How could he love me in too-big clothes that barely fit?
I wish my curves knew which way to go.
I wish I could live my body without being called a hoe.
The truth is I hate my body and I hate the way I look.
I hate my smile. I hate the way my lips form a weird hook.
I hate almost everything about me. I wish I could snap my fingers and Change.
I feel fat and unpretty so I cried extra hard today.

' Healing Together '

From the bottom of my heart, I apologize.

For making the tears fall from your beautiful eyes.

I never had the intention to abandon you when you needed me most

It was hard to not have you here, I wasn't sure how to cope

I hope you find it in your heart to forgive me.

Hopefully, together we can work on healing.

I never meant for you to feel like a burden.

I'm my defense, you weren't the only one hurting.

I know what real love is because of you.

However, admitting my feelings isn't something I'm accustomed to.

I hate the thought of you feeling this rage.

Looking over your shoulder, waiting on the day.

The day they say you're free. Physically and mentally.

I'd write you a thousand poems just to tell you what's meant to be.

You are the only man that knows me without ever being inside.

I have so much love for you, but it's sometimes outweighed by pride.

When everybody turned their back on you, I was supposed to be there.

To love you and nurture you, to show that I care.

I was foolish to ever had met you go.

You mean the world to me. I'll let whoever knows.

I still have doubts that when your time is up you'll be done with this.

You'll want to have fun, no time for a relationship.

You have my heart forever. No matter how hard I try to hide it.

There's always been a hole there. It seems you are the perfect fit.

Allow me to fix what I have broken.

I just ask that you keep your mind open and us be patient with each other while we deal with these emotions.

I can't bear to watch you love anyone else so I have to be better for you.

'Thought Process '

My thoughts have been hard to process lately.
I'm not even sure if it's me that's thinking.
I can't hear much of them over the music I'm drowning in.
I can't feel my pain through the smoke I'm breathing in.
When the music's down and the smoke clears
I'm forced to face the worst of my fears.
What if there was a way to die and still be alive?
What if I could not feel anything and still be able to cry?
Help me to overcome this depression.
I'm talking to myself better yet the soul in question.
I'm lost in this world, I fear I don't belong.
Even in my own house, I feel I'm not at home.
My heart wants love and my mind wants peace.
My body wants sex, my soul wishes for all of our ashes to
be spread at the beach.
Too young to dream of death.
Too proud to ask for help.
Dark shadows hang over my head.
Just like the feeling of me being dead.
What if I'm gone and they come to find me?
Revive me, I'm forced to live, to keep trying.
Is this life shit not hard enough?
Why the fuck my mental gotta be so rough.
Why I gotta think like this?
Feeling like I'm swimming in the devil's piss.
Why can't my mom accept who I am?
She always acts like she doesn't give a damn.
What's the point of this poem?
I guess I'm just venting.
Trying to explain this dump I've been living in.

' Time Concept '

My concept of time has slowly started to fleet
I feel as if I'm living the same days over on repeat
Constantly working. Making my mind and body weak.
Putting different things in front of me so I forget to think.
Facing the thoughts inside my head is a logical fear.
The louder these thoughts, make my cause of death clear.
I'll be drowned with thoughts of anxiety.
The feeling of loneliness is eating me alive quietly.
Lately, I haven't been feeling like myself.
My mind is in bondage and need of help.
I want to self-medicate and become my therapist.
What I truly need is a professional analysis.
I am shattered inside and I cannot find the source.
The voice in my head cried out but it is now become horse.
Raspy, dysfunctional and violent.
My heart bleeds and will stop beating to its content.
My happiness has faded.
My precious time has been wasted.
My tears and my feelings make me anxious.
I'm now familiar with whoever it is I see
I do not know this girl. This time it is not me.
Confused and still broken.
She seems dazed. She's not at all coping.
I've lost the me I was trying to find.
Just like I lost hope in love and the fear of dying.
Just like I've lost the concept of time.

' Soulties Pt 1 '

How can my heart still love you after everything you've done for me?

How can the deepest parts of me still feel like we are meant to be?

I gave you my soul but made you promise to cherish it.

And at first, you did, even made promises to marry it.

And now my heart is broken and my soul is in pain?

Tears come to my eyes every time I think of you or hear your name.

My biggest fear with us was that I always knew you would leave me one day.

I stressed this to you over and over again, each time you promised to stay.

And that's what's hurting me the most because I believed you.

You made me feel so safe every word you said had to be true.

I had bad feelings but I chose not to listen.

This is what I get for disregarding my intuition.

You were my everything and you were so perfect.

Pain in my chest as I scream out and cry.

Smoke in my lungs as I stare at the sky.

' Inside the Nympho '

As my brain wanders off, flashbacks flood my mind.
Making every part of my body anticipate the next time.
Lately, I've been craving your body heat.
Feening to mess up what was neat.
I love the way you kiss me from the neck to below the navel.
Bend me in any way that you see fit and able.
I love the way you part my lips with your tongue and kiss me after.
This time around my body's the slave and you're the master.
You let me taste the mess we just made.
The images in my head are what we've portrayed.
I love the look on your face as you watch my treasure pulsate and my chest and body heave.
What gets me going is just the thought of you watching me.
In my ear, your soft moans are heaven.
As they get louder the more the bed wettens.
I love the feeling of you pushing deep inside my paradise
I love to hear the outbursts when we lock eyes.
You like to grab the places I hate.
Licking and kissing like you're finishing your plate.
You're my body's new high.
Fucking me better than any guy.
Making me explode numerous times, most at your demand.
Once in a while, on my ass, the print of your hand.
Your voice makes me drip and convulse.
Deep down in my gut, there's a quick pulse.
Whether you tell me to hold it on or let it out.
It's tantalizing and I can't help but shout.
Your breathing quickens .and you speed up a little.
Just to slow back down and release in the middle.
As I make it to the end I sing you're name.
I look at you and smile because I'm glad we came.

' Soulties pt 2 '

Even as I lay and write this letter to you, tears flow from my eyes.

My heart has been hurting so bad I'll take almost any drug to heal the pain.

After all, a trip while I'm still here is the only thing keeping me from driving myself insane.

Sometimes I don't even want to write because I'm terrified of what my heart has to say.

It makes no sense, how you broke me to pieces and I still wish you stayed.

It wasn't too late just yet we could have worked it out.

Although in the back of my mind, the question of your loyalty would always be a doubt.

Finally letting this out gives my brain a little reassurance.

I'm going to be okay, it's just myself I have to nourish.

I hate that you hurt me, however, I wish you no harm.

I still secretly pray God will bring you back to my arms.

Every fiber of my being knows it's time to let go.

I can't bring myself to do it just yet. There are things I just have to know.

Like what, how, and mainly why?

How could you hold the deepest part of my soul,

And still, look at me in the eyes and LIE?

I TRUSTED YOU! I LOVED YOU! I FUCKING NEEDED YOU!

Somebody tell me how the FUCK do I break this SOULTIE..

' Drugs and tattoos pt1 '

There are times when even the music gives me
anxiety
When I can't decide whats inside of me
What emotions will control me today
Why does my brain always have so much to say
There are so many reasons I just want to be calm
But so many things make me anxious, they are
hard to run from
The things I should have been taught, are
teaching me.
So many cries for help cover my body
Better Than me slitting my wrist and crying
Speaking of, why am I not afraid of dying
Is it because of the brokenness in my head
Trying to find new escapes to indulge in
Now I'm forced to see things that need to be
healed.
From stolen souls to broken hearts
To those who hide inside their art
They and I are one and the same
Only, I write it down so the paper feels my pain.

' Drugz & Tattoos pt2 '

And with honor, it takes the pain away from me
Kinda how the stress leaves with the weed.
I'm losing connections I sought to have forever.
Fighting for relationships only I want to be a better
Wicked thoughts are beginning to creep back in.
Slowly questioning everyone I call a friend.
Is it that time of year again?
When days are short as nights get longer.
When just like the wind my heart grows colder.
Is THIS depression seasonal or reasonable?
How can you not know who to love?
And deny you being gay?
Is it because like your love for women,
Your happiness isn't every day?
And your sadness is more often than not.
People can't see your emotions through the smoke.
Meanwhile, you sit and watch, wishing you could choke.
I had that sweet vision again.
The one of blood dripping.
Leaving my arm.
The result of self-harm.
Instead, I roll up and get a tattoo.
To cover up the scars I'm hiding from you.

' Suicide Note '

11 cuts across the skin.
Trying to make a quick end.
I don't want to live anymore. I don't want to feel shit.
I'm sorry momma if you ever end up reading this.
I'm broken inside. And now scarred on the out.
Overthinking and filling my head with doubts.
I just want to drown and eventually in up in the clouds.
It'd be better without me here.
You guys don't need me near.
And when I finally get the courage to finish me off.
Don't cry for me. This isn't a loss.
It's a gain.
I'm no longer in pain.
Try to remain calm. Don't take it out on anyone.
It isn't their fault I'm gone.
I tried to cry for help for years.
Everybody acted as if they couldn't hear.
Clawing at my chest asking god to help me.
Depression must be a sin because I feel so deadly.
I don't want to feel this pain I want to go numb.
I was tired of pretending to be happy. It made me feel dumb.
Let me drift into the darkness.
Let my body be lifeless when you walk in.
Don't try to bring me back
This is hell where my mind is at.
I've locked myself in the room and cried my eyes out.
Not once have you ever heard me shout?
Only cause you weren't paying attention.
Only cause you never listen.
I'm hurting can't you tell ?!
No, you can't because the smile hides it well.
I'm never enough for anybody.
Not even myself. But that's obvious. Oddly.
I wish the scarves in my closet were strong enough to hold.
I wish I was short enough to hang from the ceiling mold.
I keep thinking of the relief if you find me.
Maybe in the car or the bathtub bleeding.
These are sick thoughts.
But they make me feel better off.
So much more I want to write.
But I don't wish to send your heart into fright.
If I didn't wake up tomorrow that would be fine
You guys will be happy. I know you've been trying

' To My Mother '

Sometimes we form thoughts from a loss of hope
Sometimes we use emotions to help us cope
In all reality, everything we go through makes us stronger
Give us will power to hang on a little longer
Your smile is as bright as seven suns
Your heart as pure as newborn lungs
You are the backbone and the strength of this foundation
Filling in the places wherever we fall weak in
You are our queen
Your matriarchy
You are the balance even in a catastrophe
You are my reason
For love and to keep believing
Protectiveness runs through your veins
As past events have left their stains
You are an official sacrifice
Giving all of your love as another's prize
You are a jewel and we must protect you
Keeping you away from all harmful things
Even though sometimes the mind is our greatest enemy
We can not feed into its sorrowful energy
I know that time can get weary and rough
But your healing words are always enough
You make others smile even though you are hurting
But it's the kindness in your heart that is working
You are the most beautiful intelligent person I've ever seen
In this poem to me, this is what mother means

' Being Alone '

I've begun to love being alone.

With only my energy to set the tone.

I never realized how loud the world is until the music stopped.

I never knew what heartache was until my heart dropped.

Your words are so loud but your vibration is so low.

All the negativity is blocking your room to grow.

As I said before I'm vibrating at a different frequency.

So lower your voice but still speak highly when you speak to me

' Pudge '

Today I laughed when I saw my lil pudge
You know from being on vacation and eating too much
Small enough to let my pants slip a little
Big enough so they don't fall.
With the laugh, I saw joy, 'cause I'm taking back my power.
Learned that I'm delicate but I am no one's flower.
I'm not to be given as a reward, an apology, or even a token of love.
And I'm not the dryer setting you turn to when your clothes need to fit like a glove.
Instead, I am the sacred treasure the people prayed to their ancestors for.
Being loved by me is having all the gold you can hold and more.
Access was taken for granted so now the treasure is hidden.
Locked away in my chest, no access, trespassers are forbidden.
So again I laughed today when I saw my cute little pudge.
Because if I'm the only one with access, then I'm the only one with the right to judge
And what about me could I possibly detest?
I'm Gorgeous as fuck, a Goddess nonetheless.

' Open '

I'm not shutting you out on purpose
I'm shutting you out because I'm hurting
And when I'm hurting I feel like you'd only hurt me more
When I'm hurting like this my connection with God feels so poor
I can't let you see me upset
I can't let you know you hurt me
You're just going to ask me to explain but I've never been that open
I start praying for a miracle hoping things may change
Cause I tend to hurt people when I feel this way
Closing myself up in darkness
Hoping to decay the hardness,
The coldness of my heart
But it only makes it worse so here we are, at the start.
Where do we even begin?
For construction is not finished.
It just stopped a little suddenly.
Making it hard to find the opening.
I can't stay in here for long, I'm deteriorating
I'm trying so hard to stop myself from hating
I don't want to shut down
Clutching my chest as I fall to the ground
In pain, this must be my anxiety
Or possibly the bitterness living inside me.
Depression doesn't seem to go away
Just hide for a while and wait for a good day.
If I've ever cried to you I was at my weakest
Because I wipe my tears away, I can't let you see this
I don't want to talk about it with you so don't even try
If I open up to wide I just might cry
Oh how badly I want to let the darkness take me back in
Slide the blade back across my wrist wishing to die again
It's cold in here and no blanket can help it
I won't tell you how I feel because you'll call me selfish
You'll see my mental issues as no big deal
And you wouldn't even try to help me heal

Continued on next page...

You'll push my feelings to the back of your mind
And me? I'll sit beside you and be wishing to die inside
But I'll cover it up with a sheer smile
Pretend to be happy for a while
But even in your presence
You wouldn't know the difference
Of a smile that is forced
And smiling in rejoice
Not being able to handle bad dreams
I toss, turn, and cower in my sleep
But when I am awake
I feel the world I can overtake
Not healthy for me to hurt so deeply within
Also not safe for me to keep the door open
You'll toy with my emotion on strings
Like contortion dolls, you see on screens
I'm hoping one day I find peace
I turn over and just wallow in my sheets
I don't want to eat, please don't feed me.
I don't want to talk, please don't read me.
I just want to sleep, please just leave me.
Leave me alone
Enjoy your ride home
Don't turn back
Just let your mind roam
This may very well be a cry for help
A sort of loud, yet quiet Yelp
Imagine the hurt and pain as heartache I've been feeling
To give in, open up, and let you come near me
This story can't be finished, it has to be more
I'm sore, it's raining, I'm cold, I'm scared...
Please,please , please ...open the door

' Open Pt2 '

In effort to hide from my emotions
Sometimes I'll refrain from being so open.
Being open and letting it out gets you hurt.
But keeping it inside makes it 10 times worse.
The feeling in my chest,
Cancels out the feeling of progress.
I still feel lonely and undeserving
Trying to distract myself, but it's just not working.
What good am I if I'm still broken?
How am I supposed to heal if my heart will not open?
I shut everyone out cause I feel I'm better alone.
And in my mind, depression has made me a home.
Things I try so desperately to fight,
Only find a way to take over during the night.
Crying tears that seemed almost impossible
Putting all my emotions into a sealed bottle.
It's hard to fall in love again, it's hard to show emotions.
How can I let them in if my heart will not open?

' Inside my head '

It comes over me like a wave.

Burns inside me like a blaze.

The tears break through and began to stream down my face.

I wonder why I'm not enough or why am I built this way.

Why am I so guarded?

Why is my heart so hardened?

Beginning to feel like I need people cause I'm starting to feel alone.

But when I'm around people I still don't feel at home.

Why does it have to be like this?

Why does my mind slip into the abyss?

Why does it hurt to let people in?

Why am I never able to be open?

My body begins to feel like what's going on inside my head.

Thoughts of the world being a better place if someone found me dead.

It hurts to think like this I know I shouldn't be.

But this depression has me feeling like nobody loves me.

I know it's hereditary and I wish to break the chain.

And I'm trying to just so many crossed wires in my brain

' Session 2 '

Do you know how it feels to float?

While wearing sadness on you, a heavy coat?

"I see it's just you today, how about you tell me what's been going on?"

I feel like every time I try to do something good every thing just goes wrong.

Like why am I wired this way?

Why do I think like this?

Why is it that every other day I'm having anxiety tics?

"I'm sure we will figure it out, no need to be upset."

But what if you can't help me? What if you're just like the rest?

"Isn't that what life's about? Taking risks?"

Fuck this I can't take it!

I'm done with this shit.

' Late thoughts '

Seems as though now, my thoughts only express themselves through tears.
My poems are unfinished just like the task of overcoming my fears.
Fear of rejection, afraid of negligence, and abandonment
People hurt me and in my heart, I build a wall of ice and resentment.
I begin to wonder what on earth could be wrong with me.
Lovely to be around but for some reason they always leave.
I want bonds I don't have to fight for
Love that doesn't leave my heart sore.
Look me in the eyes and tell me what part of my soul are you viewing.
Do you see my desires, my passions, or even the dreams I'm pursuing
Are you blinded by the light my soul is made of?
Or attracted to the darkness which some of us love.
Inside I feel as though I burn as bright as a million suns.
But I'll just get to the point no metaphors or silly puns.
This battle I'm fighting seems to have no end.
No white flags, a battle buddy, or even a friend.
I'm at war with myself. My soul is under attack.
And if I let the evil win, there's no way I'll get it back.
I want to be seen, what's-more understood.
I wish to be loved, for I am all things good.
There is no good without evil so I guess there's a balance.
If earning my heart was a sport, who would partake in the challenge?
I know the kind of love I give, I know exactly what I want, and I know exactly who I am.
Or at least I think I do, lines get blurred when I'm laid under a man.
As if I need him to tell me how pretty my eyes are or how sexy I am.
He doesn't even know the value of the jewel he holds in his hands.
I'm made of Rare jewel, not many can't have or hold it.
And to gain my trust so many claimed to be solid but folded.
Conversation with myself to see if I'm crazy.
Therapy sessions go on here daily.
At the end of the day, who can I talk to, the wall?
Well, there's no judgment, it's quiet, and maybe it'll listen after all.
Does the pain change a person? How would you know?
If this heart has been broken, how could it grow?
I assume it's like a flower, you may just need to nurture it.
But like a daisy in the rose bush, I just don't fit.
Not into your quotas or standards of what you think I should be like.
When the sun goes down and I'm alone Is when the shit in my head decides to strike.
Are we dying to live? Or living to survive?
Not the way I'm feeling, hell no this can't be life.
I refuse to accept it, don't I deserve peace?
Why even bother with this shit I'll just let it be.

' A Scarred Heart '

A scar is a reminder of the pain that's not there but once was.

However, the scars on my heart are reopening and pouring out blood.

The cuts will heal but the scars will take time to fade away.

And without realizing you'll look and it'll be gone one day.

Can you call it a scar if the wound isn't healed?

If the cuts burst back open every time you decide to feel?

I roll my pain in a backwood just to help me cope.

Wanting to feel numb. In fear, I've lost hope.

I'm in fear that I've also lost love.

My heart weeps violently asking for help from above.

New Tears in my heart will take time to scar.

Scar tissue will be way thicker making it hard for them to be ajar.

Can a scarred heart still bleed?

As long as a broken heart can still beat.

' Seasons '

They say that love is like the seasons.

If that's true then soon you'll be leaving

In autumn, like the leaves, you'll fall in love.

By the time summer comes around, like the fallen leaves, you'll be gone.

I don't understand, and I don't want to hurt you.

I feel my winter is far too cold for you to run into.

And I don't want to be sprung on the idea of fairy tales.

And here comes the summer again, I know this heat all too well.

' Broke me. '

I know that what we had wasn't real.

But I'm stuck on what was and trying to heal.

How do I get over you when I fell so hard so fast?

I thought the love I gave you would be enough to make things last.

You were my first feeling of something new

How could I not be attached to you?

How come you changed on me like that?

How come you never saw a problem with the tough guy act?

I loved you. I wanted you. I needed you. I cared.

How could you leave me after promising you'd be there?

You broke me worse than anyone else.

I told you I was hurt and you told me you'd help.

What am I supposed to do to move on?

You were the one I fiend for but the other girl won.

What was it? What changed? You said you loved me and I said the same.

' And again '

And again my heart is sore
Because people weren't enough people and I was so much more.
And again, my mind is in a frenzy.
Feel again like the world is against me.
How many times can one's heartbreak?
All that I gave was all that they'd take.
And again, my heart is sore.
This time way more blood drips on the floor.
This time rage takes over my body.
I released a side only I knew was inside me.
Smashing mirrors and breaking things.
Realizing I've become some sort of fling
Why not just leave, I asked if you needed to.
Why keep me around, what's this leading to?
I hurt for you, I cried with you.
I can't help but think this is all my fault.
Somehow I messed up, somehow I failed
We came in too hot and crashed down
And along the way, my heart sank into the ground.
And again my heart is sore.
And again, I'm left alone.
And again my pain is seeping out of my eyes.
In the form of rivers coming from my cries.
And again I was too open.
And again I'm back to coping
And again I wish to be numb.
And again I'm made to feel dumb.
And again I plan to hide the pain,
With a slew of drugs and alcohol to keep me sane.
And again I'm left to heal from the things I thought were real.

' Wasted love '

Now. When I think about this love shit
It starts to seem ridiculous
Thinking about shit to do for you or what to say when we kick it
I'm kinda pissed off cause you were fucking up my image
But now it's your loss cause Ian fell back in with it
Keep your distance,im sure karma will hit.
I feel bad for whatever shorty falls for you next
You won't do shit but use her for money & sex...
For a minute you will fuck with her mind
Get some pussy from her to boost yo pride
After a while, she'll fall in love and you'll toss her to the side
SMH.
FUCK YOU NIGGA. And I mean that shit sincerely.
You played with my heart and that's the greatest thing with in me.
What's crazy is, I held you up when you were down.
But you let that go cause you wanna fuck around?!
You dumb ass nigga what the fuck were you thinking?!
Like I wasn't the shit?!
Like I wasn't worth more than keeping?!

' Session 4 '

" Good evening my dear , late night it's been a while.
For a moment I thought I'd seen you smile.
And suddenly it feels we're back to square one?
What do you make of what your mental state has become?
You've lost yourself again? After all you're here to see me .
A mental image of the therapist you actually need to see.
You cannot rope yourself through these things .
You cannot put your time into such flings.
I'm going to prescribe you some drugs to take .
Just to ease your mind whenever you're awake .
You're quiet , do have anything say?
I refuse to let you sit and wallow away.
Depression and heart break has its end .
Sometimes the healing starts from with in.
Relearn to love yourself , think of you as...a friend. "

' And now '

And now, here I am stressing.

For that deeper connection.

My mind is always racing and I'm so tired of stressing.

Hiding my hurt behind forced smiles and straight faces.

Allowing my heart to drag my mind to dear places.

All in all, I just want to know what it's worth.

All of the love I gave you and you just left me hurt.

Unconditionally I cared for you.

And in my heart I wanted this to be true.

This pain is starting to show physically.

Drowning in depression and sorrow mentally.

' Learning To Live'

Do we live as long as we learn, or do we learn as long as we live?

We are the ones who give our all, even when there's nothing else to give.

We feel unappreciated and unwanted.

We feel unworthy of love but that's how they want it.

Although everything hurts. From our heads to our hearts.

Scared of redoing this, but in need of a fresh start.

So we take it to the chin and keep on pressing.

Praying to the sky or pain is way less than our blessing.

Who can we love if we don't love ourselves?

This time our happiness matters and nothing else.

' Under Construction '

I guess it took some time, but you can say I'm healing now
I needed you out my life but I couldn't see how.
How I was going to live without you or try to move on
Then I realized I was hurting for too long
So many nights I cried, wishing to meet your expectations
And yet when you called me my heart got to racing
I couldn't tell what it was but I should've let you go
Cause now that you're gone I'm starting to see a slight glow
Retraining my heart to love and my face to smile.
Gaining a humility that was much needed after a while
I'd grown so angry with you and so hot-headed
Relationships and friends became something I dreaded
Now I'm opening myself to new opportunities
Some that have been right in front of me
Analyzing our situation and calling myself stupid
But no, I'd just been struck by Cupid
Foolish of me to lose myself in you
Stressing about all the things that you do.
Waking myself up from the post-traumatic heartbroken haze
How ironic, the prettiest flowers have seen the darkest days
Now that I'm under construction, becoming and new person
Your hold on me can no longer worsen
Only grow pathetic and what's more weak
As the light in me climbs to its peak
I guess I should thank you though, for every heartache pain and tear
You made a me I never knew was there
Why is it that you like to hurt these girls
After telling them they were your whole world
Guys like you turn girls into hoes
But not me, my heart just grew a little cold
Never forget, a blessing is on the horizon
On my face, a smile is something surprising
After being asked why I couldn't show emotion,
I took the ones you gave me and tossed them in the ocean
Yellow tape, not for murder but for construction
They'll be astonished at this new production
And farewell to all times of destruction,
Because now it's my time and I'm coming out flourishing

' I am the Art '

In light of many nights passing, I look around and find myself asking,

What's going to be left of me when I leave?

So I created this art that tells my story.

Leaving it here for when I'm called to glory.`

My story is here for you and others.

When you finish it please comfort my mother.

I am the art, the artist, and the fashion.

I am the poetry, the poet, and the classics.

My art was created differently and took longer to dry.

My art will pierce your heart.

And tears you will cry.

I am the art, the artist, and the fashion.

Here is my art in a story for those who want to know what happened.

My art is full of love and obsession.

Strong will versus pain and depression.

I hope you can relate, if not just pass it on.

However, I AM the Art and my story will live on.

Dedication
I dedicate this book to those who believe in me. A special
thanks to my brothers and sisters who pushed me to put
this book. And also to those of you who read my words
with empathy, or saw that these precious words resonate
with your feelings.
It is not always easy to express how you feel. However,
the poems in this book are merely evidence of my
humility.

Thanks For Reading.

Thank You.

Made in the USA
Middletown, DE
31 August 2023

37693813R00029